Participant Guide
THIRD EDITION

What's My
Communication
Style?

Developed by:

Eileen M. Russo, PhD

Assisted by:

Stephanie McBrier Hannett, PhD

Deborah Topka, MS

For additional copies of this publication, contact the HRDQ Client Services Team at:

Phone: 800-633-4533
        610-279-2002

Fax: 800-633-3683
        610-279-0524

Online: HRDQ.com

ISBN: 978-1-58854-674-6

Publisher: Martin Delahoussaye
Editorial Development: Michael McIrvin; Charyl Leister
Publishing Assistant: Sarah Grey
Interior Design: Laura Shaffert; Mark Pendleton
Cover Design: Doug Todd

 Printed in the United States of America.

EN-03-MR-11

What's *Your* Communication Style?

What's My Communication Style? will provide you with new insight into your everyday communications with others. This assessment offers an accurate and reliable way to quickly identify your communication style. It will also help you understand the various forms of communication, identify the communication styles of others, and learn how to "flex" your style to improve communication.

• •

Taking and Scoring the Assessment

Determining Your Communication Style Profile

Taking and Scoring the Assessment

For each item on the following pages, select the statement ending that reflects the way you communicate. Sometimes you will find that more than one statement describes you. In that case, choose the one that most closely reflects your communication behavior. As you answer each question, put an "X" in the box of the corresponding letter on the enclosed Response Form as shown below in Figure 1.

Figure 1: What's My Communication Style? Response Form

What's My Communication Style?

Directions: The letters a, b, c, and d in each of the 24 boxes below correspond with the endings of the 24 statements in the *What's My Communication Style?* assessment. Carefully read each statement and then mark an 'X' in the box alongside the letter that most closely reflects your behavior.

1	7	13	19
a ☐	a ☐	a ☐	a ☐
b ☐	b ☐	b ☐	b ☐
c ☐	c ☐	c ☐	c ☐
d ☐	d ☐	d ☐	d ☐
2	**8**	**14**	**20**
a ☐	a ☐	a ☐	a ☐
b ☐	b ☐	b ☐	b ☐
c ☐	c ☐	c ☐	c ☐
d ☐	d ☐	d ☐	d ☐
3	**9**	**15**	**21**
a ☐	a ☐	a ☐	a ☐
b ☐	b ☐	b ☐	b ☐
c ☐	c ☐	c ☐	c ☐
d ☐	d ☐	d ☐	d ☐
4	**10**	**16**	**22**
a ☐	a ☐	a ☐	a ☐
b ☐	b ☐	b ☐	b ☐
c ☐	c ☐	c ☐	c ☐
d ☐	d ☐	d ☐	d ☐
5	**11**	**17**	**23**
a ☐	a ☐	a ☐	a ☐
b ☐	b ☐	b ☐	b ☐
c ☐	c ☐	c ☐	c ☐
d ☐	d ☐	d ☐	d ☐
6	**12**	**18**	**24**
a ☐	a ☐	a ☐	a ☐
b ☐	b ☐	b ☐	b ☐
c ☐	c ☐	c ☐	c ☐
d ☐	d ☐	d ☐	d ☐

What's My Communication Style? Third Edition

1. **When I am in a meeting, I prefer to sit …**
   a. at the head of the table.
   b. where people can see me.
   c. directly next to another person.
   d. with at least one seat between me and the next person.

2. **When I speak with a person, I …**
   a. look down sometimes.
   b. look directly at him or her the entire time.
   c. look at him or her often.
   d. tend to look around the room more than at the person.

3. **When I greet people I know fairly well, I …**
   a. say hello but do not touch them.
   b. give them a firm handshake.
   c. give them a hug.
   d. give them an enthusiastic handshake.

4. **When I am talking to people, I …**
   a. like to stand close to them.
   b. feel uncomfortable if they stand too close to me.
   c. get annoyed when they stand too close.
   d. don't mind if they are close to me.

5. **My walk is …**
   a. slow and leisurely.
   b. lively.
   c. even.
   d. hasty.

6. **When other people talk, I …**
   a. look for the main point.
   b. look for a good story.
   c. look for supporting facts.
   d. try to figure out their feelings.

7. When I speak publicly, I …

a. vary my voice level for effect.

b. speak clearly but not loudly.

c. speak relatively quietly.

d. speak in loud tones.

8. When I see conflict, I …

a. try to lighten the mood by focusing on the positive.

b. avoid it.

c. dive right in.

d. try to figure out what caused it.

9. When people enter my workspace, I …

a. ask them if they would like to sit down.

b. tell them to sit down.

c. let them decide where or if to take a seat.

d. pull out a chair for them.

10. When I am engaged in problem solving, I …

a. lead the discussion.

b. listen to what other people have to say.

c. focus on the big picture.

d. focus on the facts.

11. I usually start conversations by …

a. finding out how the other person's day is going.

b. telling a story.

c. jumping right into the subject.

d. establishing the purpose of the conversation.

12. When I make a decision, I …

a. see how other people are going to be affected by it.

b. rely on my own judgment.

c. look for others' approval of my decision.

d. rely on sound decision-making methods.

13. When someone is giving a presentation, I …

a. need it to be entertaining.

b. imagine how he or she must feel.

c. try to evaluate the logic of it.

d. get impatient if it is not fast-moving.

14. When acquaintances touch me (e.g., put their hand on my arm), I …

a. welcome it.

b. become irritated.

c. feel closer to them.

d. feel uncomfortable.

15. When I am trying to get what I want, I …

a. can tap into others' wants and needs.

b. make a strong argument for my case.

c. have a great sales pitch.

d. am cool and competent.

16. In terms of how others see me, I …

a. control what they learn about me.

b. let others know how I feel.

c. am a private person.

d. am an open book.

17. In a group meeting, I …

a. tend to evaluate ideas.

b. keep everyone involved.

c. tend to take responsibility for leading the conversation.

d. listen carefully to what people want.

18. As far as I am concerned, public expression of personal feelings …

a. makes things more interesting.

b. makes people somewhat uncomfortable.

c. helps me to interact with others.

d. gets in the way of getting work done.

19. My intent in a business meeting is to …

a. get my opinions across.

b. build a relationship with others.

c. persuade others.

d. investigate the situation.

20. When I tell a story, I …

a. focus on the characters' personal situations.

b. keep people on the edge of their seats.

c. systematically build a case.

d. get right to the point.

21. In terms of teamwork, I …

a. support the team.

b. prefer to take responsibility myself rather than rely on a team.

c. easily grow impatient with it.

d. rally the team.

22. When I give a presentation, it …

a. is well organized.

b. taps into people's emotions.

c. is forceful.

d. is entertaining.

23. When people get upset or cry in front of me, I …

a. prefer to stop them.

b. try to counsel them.

c. try to cheer them up.

d. try to think of ways to remove myself from the situation.

24. My telephone calls …

a. are as brief as possible.

b. focus only on the business at hand.

c. are lively.

d. tend to be long.

Determining Your Communication Style Profile

Step 1: Use a pencil or pen to separate the Response Form and the Scoring Form.

Step 2: Count the number of times you put an "X" for each style shape and place the resulting totals in the corresponding "Style Total" shapes on the Scoring Form.

Step 3: Copy each of the Style Totals into the corresponding shapes on Figure 2 below.

Step 4: Determine which of the four Style Totals has the highest score. Write the name of this style in the "My dominant style is:" box at the bottom of the page. If the results indicate that two or more styles scored the highest, include each of them.

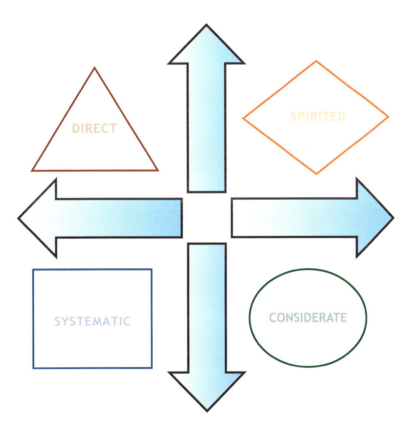

Figure 2: Your Communication Style Profile

Your communication style comes through whether or not you are aware of it. The style that you use most often is called your dominant style. Dominant styles are typically indicated by scores of 9 or higher.

My dominant style is: _____

What Is Communication Style?

Most people think of communication as a verbal or written exchange between two or more people. However, you will soon discover that it is far more complex than this simple perception. In addition to what we say, communication involves how we say it, what our body language conveys, and even how we organize our personal space.

· ·

Four Types of Communication

Two Dimensions of Communication Style

Four Types of Communication

Communication is complicated because it includes more than just the spoken or written word. *What's My Communication Style?* focuses on four different forms of communication: verbal, paraverbal, body language, and personal space. Each of these elements adds a layer of complexity to communication.

Verbal

You have complete control over the words you use in a statement, but the meaning of those words may not be shared by the person with whom you are speaking. Differences in age, experience, and background can result in differing interpretations of the same statement. The better you understand both your own style and the styles of others, the better you can adapt your communication.

Paraverbal

It is not just the words you say but also the way you say them that communicates meaning. This is called paraverbal communication and it includes how quickly one speaks and pauses, as well as voice tone and intensity.

Paraverbal cues help you interpret the meaning of what someone is saying. Without these cues, you would be unable to interpret speech forms such as sarcasm. Taking turns in conversation is also determined by paraverbal cues. When someone trails off or lowers his voice, that can be a sign it is the other party's turn to speak.

Like verbal communication, a mismatch of styles can make interpretation more difficult, and consequently, understanding communication styles can enhance reception.

Body Language

The way you stand, shake hands, and maintain eye contact are all forms of body language that communicate meaning to others. Body language can communicate attentiveness, emotions, and reactions. Facial expressions are another form of body language. The cliché "It's written all over your face" says it all: your facial expressions can reveal your true response to what someone says even before you formulate a response in words.

Body language is also heavily influenced by your communication style. Preferences for eye contact, gesturing, and touch are usually quite pronounced and it is easier to read another person's body language message if you know her style.

Personal Space

The final type of communication is the use of personal space, which includes not only the space between you and others, but also your personal appearance, your choice of decorations, and how you arrange your workspace. Interpersonal distance, or how close people are physically to one another, has been studied extensively, and researchers have outlined four zones of interpersonal distance: intimate, personal, social, and public. How close you prefer to be to others in all of these zones is a function of your communication style. Whether your work or home space is cluttered or neat, organized or disorganized is also a function of your communication style.

All four forms of communication play a role in our ability to send messages. Verbal communication is the most easily controlled form, but it is important to think about how you use the other forms of communication and how others are interpreting your messages. It is beneficial to understand these forms of communication as a receiver of messages in order to better understand the sender's intent and motivations. Figure 3 below shows how each communication style influences the different forms of communication.

	DIRECT	**SPIRITED**	**CONSIDERATE**	**SYSTEMATIC**
Verbal	■ decisive ■ direct speech ■ doesn't stop to say hello	■ generalizes ■ persuasive ■ expresses opinions readily	■ listens ■ close, personal language ■ supportive language	■ precise language ■ avoids emotions ■ focuses on specific details
Paraverbal	■ speaks quickly ■ loud tones ■ formal speech	■ loud tones ■ animated ■ lots of voice inflection	■ speaks slowly ■ soft tones ■ patient speech	■ even delivery ■ brief speech ■ little vocal variety
Body Language	■ direct eye contact ■ bold visual appearance ■ firm handshake	■ quick actions ■ lots of body movement ■ enthusiastic handshake	■ slow movement ■ tactile ■ gentle handshake	■ poker face ■ avoids touching ■ controlled movement
Personal Space	■ keeps physical distance ■ work space suggests power ■ displays planning calendars in work space	■ cluttered workspace ■ personal slogans in office ■ likes close physical space	■ family pictures in workspace ■ likes side-by-side seating ■ carries sentimental items	■ a strong sense of personal space ■ charts, graphs in office ■ prefers an organized desktop

Figure 3: Four Types of Communication

Two Dimensions of Communication Style

Although each individual is unique, there are categorical commonalities in personality style as reflected in how we communicate. Your personality style is determined by your level of *assertiveness* and *expressiveness*.

Assertiveness is the effort that a person makes to influence or control the thoughts or actions of others. People who are assertive *tell* others how things should be and are task oriented, active, and confident. People who are less assertive *ask* others how things should be and are process oriented, deliberate, and attentive.

Expressiveness is the effort that a person makes to control his emotions when relating to others. People who are expressive display their emotions and are versatile, sociable, and demonstrative. People who are less expressive control their emotions and are focused, independent, and private.

The various combinations of the degrees of assertiveness and expressiveness result in four possible styles: *Direct*, *Spirited*, *Considerate*, and *Systematic*. These styles, shown in Figure 4, are the basis of the HRDQ Style Model.

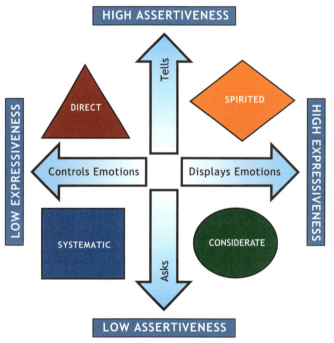

Figure 4: HRDQ Style Model

Although many people have a clearly dominant communication style, others communicate using several styles, perhaps using different styles in different situations. However, because communication takes many forms (e.g., language, facial expressions), some participants' scores might indicate greater communication flexibility.

If your dominant style score is below 9, you are probably comfortable using more than one style to communicate. If your scores indicate that you have two equally dominant styles, you probably communicate with both comfortably, perhaps switching back and forth between styles depending on the situation.

If you have three or more equally scored styles, you might communicate with all of these styles comfortably. However, it is fairly uncommon for a person to be completely comfortable using three or more communication styles, and if you suspect your scores may not be reflective of your actual communication behavior, use the charts throughout this guide to clarify your preferred style(s).

Understanding Communication Style

Knowing your communication style is useful, but it is important to learn how it drives your behavior and affects your daily interactions. Understanding the strengths and potential trouble spots of each of the four styles will help to guide your own communication and prepare you to anticipate and respond appropriately to the communication needs of others.

• •

Communication Style Strengths

Communication Style Trouble Spots

Interacting With Other Communication Styles

Applying What You've Learned

Communication Style Strengths

Each communication style has definite strengths. Knowledge of your strengths allows you to draw on them as needed and to find situations in which your strengths are a benefit. Knowledge of the strengths of others allows you to anticipate their reactions and adapt your style to respond appropriately.

Directions: Place a checkmark beside each behavior that best describes your behavior. Use the lines below to list additional positive behaviors you demonstrate.

Direct

Direct people take charge of their lives. You prefer to be in control and you are decisive in your actions. Direct people thrive on competition. You enjoy the challenge of a fight but enjoy the win even more. You maintain a fast pace as you work single-mindedly on your goals. Direct people are good in positions of authority that require independence. You possess strong leadership skills and get things done. You are not afraid to take risks to get what you want.

❏ Gets to the bottom line	❏ Prefers to be in control
❏ Speaks forcefully	❏ Tends to be decisive
❏ Maintains eye contact	❏ Thrives on competition
❏ Presents position strongly	❏ Likes to take risks

Others: _____

_____

Spirited

Spirited people are enthusiastic and friendly. You prefer to be around other people and thrive in the spotlight. You are able to generate motivation and excitement in others because of your positive focus and lively nature. Spirited people work at a fast pace because they prefer stimulation, and are well suited to high-profile positions in which public presentations are important. You are a spontaneous person who is quick and takes decisive action. You excel at building alliances and using relationships to accomplish work.

❏ Likes to be persuasive	❏ Prefers to be with other people
❏ Tends to be a good storyteller	❏ Works at a fast pace
❏ Focuses on the big picture	❏ Builds strong alliances
❏ Uses motivational speech	❏ Generates enthusiasm

Others: _____

_____

Considerate

Considerate people value warm, personal relationships. You have good counseling skills, and others come to you because you are a good listener. Considerate people are cooperative and enjoy being part of a team. You are reliable and steady, and you are always aware of others' feelings. You work best in an environment in which teamwork is essential. You are well suited for any profession that requires you to care for others.

❏ Listens well	❏ Values relationships
❏ Is a good counselor	❏ Enjoys being part of a team
❏ Uses supportive language	❏ Cares for others
❏ Builds trust	❏ Tends to be reliable and steady

Others: _____

_____

Systematic

Systematic people are accurate and objective. You prefer to make decisions based on facts, not emotions. Systematic people rely on data and are excellent problem solvers. You tend to be persistent in your analyses, maintaining a critical focus throughout your work. Systematic people are orderly and prefer to work in an organized environment with clear guidelines. You thrive in task-oriented positions that require independent work.

❏ Presents precisely	❏ Makes decisions based on facts
❏ Seeks information	❏ Excels at problem solving
❏ Speaks efficiently	❏ Prefers clear guidelines
❏ Prefers an organized desktop	❏ Works independently

Others: _____

_____

Communication Style Trouble Spots

Just as each style has strengths, each style also has potential trouble spots. These trouble spots stem from the simple fact that any good thing can become a problem if taken to an extreme.

Directions: Place a checkmark beside each trouble spot that describes your behavior. Use the lines below to list any other potential trouble spots you tend to exhibit.

Direct

Direct people may cross the line from controlling to overbearing. You like to get things done quickly. However, you might overlook fine details that can lead to mistakes. Direct people are not necessarily good at focusing on feelings, and tend to discount them as unimportant. You tend to view situations as competitive, making those around you uncomfortable and tense. Direct people may become workaholics when their strengths are carried to an extreme.

- ☐ **Is a poor listener**
- ☐ **Is impatient with others**
- ☐ **Does not heed advice**
- ☐ **Likes to argue**

- ☐ **Likes to compete**
- ☐ **Discounts feelings**
- ☐ **Overlooks details**
- ☐ **Tends to be a workaholic**

Others: _____

_____

Spirited

Spirited people tend to intensify their verbal behavior. You might exaggerate a story for effect or respond to criticism with verbal attacks. You also tend to generalize when outlining an idea, glossing over important details that might diminish enthusiastic support. Spirited people are rarely concerned with deadlines and may not manage their time effectively.

- ☐ **Does not hear details**
- ☐ **Tends to exaggerate**
- ☐ **Generalizes**
- ☐ **Can be overdramatic**

- ☐ **Responds poorly to criticism**
- ☐ **Glosses over details**
- ☐ **Tends to miss deadlines**
- ☐ **Does not manage time efficiently**

Others: _____

_____

Considerate

Considerate people tend to avoid change and prefer to do what is comfortable. You dislike conflict, often telling others what you think they want to hear. You have wants and needs that can linger under the surface until you become resentful. Interactions with others can become tense as a result.

❏ Avoids conflict   ❏ Prefers what is comfortable

❏ Gives in easily   ❏ Allows own needs to linger

❏ Keeps opinions to self   ❏ Resists change

❏ Overemphasizes feelings   ❏ Tells others what they want to hear

Others: _____

_____

Systematic

Systematic people may continually seek more information to make them feel confident. Your need for facts and data can delay decision making. You are uncomfortable with emotions and avoid expressing them at all costs. Systematic people tend to put quality and accuracy ahead of feelings, even if it might hurt others, and are often perceived as impersonal.

❏ Focuses too much on details   ❏ Puts accuracy ahead of feelings

❏ Fears personal disclosure   ❏ Tends to be impersonal

❏ Can be terse   ❏ Delays decision making

❏ Uses little variety in vocal tones   ❏ Does not take risks

Others: _____

_____

Interacting With Other Communication Styles

Misunderstandings are often a result of style differences. For example, a Spirited person and a Systematic person may have tense interactions because of the different speeds at which they make decisions. Although each of us has a predominant personality style that drives our behavior and our communication, we must learn to be flexible so that we can communicate with people whose personality styles vary from our own. The first step is to learn how to identify another person's style.

How to Speed Read Communication Style

Once you can identify another person's style, you can adapt behavior to accommodate that person. This will make that person feel more at ease, and it helps you both achieve your goals more readily. For example, it will be much easier to convince a Systematic person to accept a decision if you are armed with concrete facts rather than general impressions. Even if you are a Spirited person who prefers general impressions, it will serve you well to be flexible in this situation and offer those details.

Figure 5 below offers some clues that will help you quickly identify another person's communication style:

	DIRECT	SPIRITED	CONSIDERATE	SYSTEMATIC
Talking	▪ Gets to the point	▪ Tells good stories	▪ Doesn't offer opinions	▪ Precise
Listening	▪ Poor listener	▪ Doesn't hear details	▪ Sympathetic listener	▪ Seeks facts
Handshake	▪ Firm	▪ Enthusiastic	▪ Gentle	▪ Brief
Personal Space	▪ Maintains distance	▪ Likes to be close	▪ Tactile	▪ Avoids touching
Movement	▪ Bold	▪ Quick	▪ Slow	▪ Controlled
Workspace	▪ Suggests power	▪ Cluttered	▪ Displays photos	▪ Organized

Figure 5: Speed Reading Others' Styles

Flexing Your Communication Style

It takes some willingness and effort to expand beyond one's own style to interact with others. It is generally appreciated, however, and may make the difference between success and failure in an interaction.

Figure 6 below provides some tips to help you improve communication with any of the four styles:

DIRECT

- Focus on their goals and objectives
- Keep your relationship businesslike
- Argue facts, not personal feelings
- Be well organized in your presentations
- Ask questions directly
- Speak at a relatively fast pace

SPIRITED

- Focus on opinions and inspiring ideas
- Be supportive of their ideas
- Don't hurry the discussion
- Engage in brainstorming
- Be entertaining and fast moving
- Allow them to share their ideas freely

SYSTEMATIC

- Focus on facts, not opinions
- Be thorough and organized
- Provide data when possible
- Be precise in your presentations
- Avoid gimmicks
- Allow time for analysis

CONSIDERATE

- Focus on your relationship
- Be supportive of their feelings
- Make sure you understand their needs
- Be informal
- Maintain a relaxed pace
- Give them time to build trust in you

Figure 6: Flexing Your Communication Style

19

Applying What You've Learned

What's My Communication Style? has provided you with insight into how you communicate through language, body movement, and personal space. This information will be most useful if you plan to improve your skills by emphasizing your strengths, controlling your trouble spots, and learning how to "flex" your style. Use the following questions to reflect on what you have learned and to develop a plan to improve your interactions with others:

1. What are the positive aspects of your communication style?

2. List some examples of how your strengths have benefited you in your communication at work.

3. What can you do to strengthen these characteristics? What can you do to develop new strengths?

4. What are some of the aspects of your dominant style that may be potential trouble spots?

5. What can you do to control or avoid those potential trouble spots?

6. Which communication styles do you communicate with most effectively?

7. Which communication styles do you communicate with least effectively?

8. What specific challenges do you face in your everyday interactions?

9. What can you do to overcome these challenges now that you understand the importance of communication style?

About Us

HRDQ is a trusted developer of soft-skills learning solutions that help to improve the performance of individuals, teams, and organizations. We offer a wide range of resources and services, from ready-to-train assessments and programs to facilitator certification, custom development, and more.

Our primary audience includes corporate trainers, human resource professionals, educational institutions, and independent consultants who look to us for research-based solutions to develop key skills such as leadership, communication, coaching, and team building.

At HRDQ, we believe an experiential approach is the best catalyst for adult learning. Our unique Experiential Learning Model™ has been the core of what we do for more than 30 years. Combining the best of organizational learning theory and proven facilitation methods, with an appreciation for adult learning styles, our philosophy initiates and inspires lasting change.

800.633.4533
HRDQ.COM